First World War
and Army of Occupation
War Diary
France, Belgium and Germany

14 DIVISION
41 Infantry Brigade,
Brigade Light Trench Mortar Battery
24 July 1915 - 30 August 1916

WO95/1896/5

The Naval & Military Press Ltd
www.nmarchive.com
Published in association with The National Archives

Published by

The Naval & Military Press Ltd

Unit 10 Ridgewood Industrial Park,

Uckfield, East Sussex,

TN22 5QE England

Tel: +44 (0) 1825 749494

www.naval-military-press.com

www.nmarchive.com

This diary has been reprinted in facsimile from the original. Any imperfections are inevitably reproduced and the quality may fall short of modern type and cartographic standards.

© **Crown Copyright**
Images reproduced by permission of The National Archives, London, England, 2015.

Contents

Document type	Place/Title	Date From	Date To
Heading	1896/5		
Heading	14 Div 41 Bde 41 Trench Mortar Bty 1915 July To 1916 Aug 1596		
War Diary		24/07/1915	05/12/1915
War Diary	G.22 Central	06/12/1915	30/04/1916
War Diary	Field	04/05/1916	31/05/1916
Heading	War Diary Of 41st Trench Mortar Battery. From 1st July 1916 To 31st July 1916 Volume V		
War Diary	Field	01/07/1916	30/07/1916
Heading	War Diary Of 41st Trench Mortar Battery. From 1st August, 1916-To 31st August 1916 Volume VI		
War Diary		01/08/1916	30/08/1916

189615

~~Army Forms~~

14 DIV 41 Bde

41
Trench Mortar
Bty

1915 July to 1916 Aug

1596

WAR DIARY
or
INTELLIGENCE SUMMARY
(Erase heading not required.)

Army Form C. 2118

XLVI

41 - Fred Mor 1917

Place	Date	Hour	Summary of Events and Information	Remarks and references to Appendices
24	7	15	Leave school at Barthou and proceeded to 2nd Infy Brigade H.Q. and go for orders from G.R.O.	
25	7	15	Go with Headquarters of 157th Infantry Brigade and go to French Battn. and find positions for Sections H.Q. and transport for a "French" Battn. Relief & C.R.P. and arrange for a transport the following day.	
26	7	2 PM	Go up to Rumstaal morning and find billets for mess in large factory. Take all arms, equipment & (one billet in wagons?)	
		4 PM	Arrive at billets and make arrangements for 10 men — stop and stay that night to transport find that all billets are not yet ready — so have to go out but also stop —	EJ Brown Capt / 7/75 Cmdg 41/7/75

WAR DIARY
or
INTELLIGENCE SUMMARY

Army Form C. 2118

4/1st /4/1st French Howitzers

Place	Date	Hour	Summary of Events and Information	Remarks and references to Appendices
	26.7.15	6 PM	Go to Rouesbeek and arrange to billet in Zuun facing	
		2 PM	was hasty in G S wagon to base billet and view standing orders for detachment where it is. Same 2 detachments to trenches and two gun but have to leave one gun half way in a farm to & O C infantry Royle for haying up on new carry gun & ammunition to trenches	
	27.7.15		Work on dug out with supplies of S.A.A. and at night go back to base billet & bring up a 2" with 3 rounds ammunition	
	28.7.15		Work on dug out & continue putting in ammunition at 2 am night some firing very heavy and rifles	
	29.7.15		Work continues - two howitzers fire and one for 2 heavy	
	30.7.15	3 AM	fire four rounds 33/n with great success in enemy	
	31.7.15	2 AM	fire two rounds Summary at enemy party demonstration O C 6 PM could be Hooged & killed, good results	3/8/15
	1.8.15		fire four rounds in evening we were very hotly fired at and machine supremely of the enemy German machine fire along enemy trenches of F.B.Smith Lt	

Army Form C. 2118

WAR DIARY
or
INTELLIGENCE SUMMARY
(Erase heading not required.)

Instructions regarding War Diaries and Intelligence Summaries are contained in F. S. Regs., Part II. and the Staff Manual respectively. Title Pages will be prepared in manuscript.

Place	Date	Hour	Summary of Events and Information	Remarks and references to Appendices
Monday	2.8.15		Fired five rounds at 3pm in reply to minnenwerfer fire forward. Left the battery at 12.8 midday and moved to school at Berthen to arrange for a new bed for 2" gun. Then went to Brig. HdQtrs to get hang rests and get ammunition.	with a fathead [illegible]
Tuesday	3.8.15		Returned to Berthen and find Charge rounds have been fired in my absence at a working party. Went to bed for 2" to Flanders and fire two rounds.	
Wednesday	4.8.15		Fire five rounds at 6PM and Flanders owing to trees surrounding the battery and nearly every shell was out of fire were duds. Facting was high enough. There each shell that came thro' these lines was a caused a slow burning 15 gun firing.	
Thursday	5.8.15		Fired two rounds at 2 am in reply to German trenchstrap. Co-operate with Heavy howitzers at 3.30 am with Merovis from 18", 4½" howitzer. Excellent results except for the fact that 5 of the rounds were duds. Replied to whizz bangs at 11 am with 5 rounds. One round 2nd fires at 4 pm silenced the enemy's whizz bangs. Three 3 rounds from 18" at 6.30 in reply to the enemy's first of enemy whizz bangs. They last round of the three was a dud.	
Friday	6.8.15		Brought up ammunition from Wats at 1am. Fired 18 rounds with 13 inch Howitzer at 5.30 pm in operation with the heavy howitzers. Burst range was close to the enemy dugouts. One of the rounds a 33pd did not explode. The 9 pm fired 3 18" rounds in reply to the German minnenwerfer, silenceing them effectively.	

Place	Date	Hour	Summary of Events and Information	Remarks and references to Appendices
Saturday	7.8.15		Fired two rounds from the 2 inch gun at 8.30 a.m. in reply to German trench mortar. Unfortunately both failed to explode. Altered the bed of trench mortar to get in range of German loophole. G.L & A.m. gun 3 rounds reply to trench mortar. One of these was a dud.	
Sunday	8.8.15		Quiet day owing to husbanding ammunition. Situation now is that we have one gun in action in 137 Bde and 2 in 138 Bde. A Captain has been attached to 137 G and matters just I believe means a lot of work.	

R.B. Bromfield 2/Lt
comdg 4th T.H.B
8/8/15.

WAR DIARY or INTELLIGENCE SUMMARY

Army Form C. 2118

(Erase heading not required.)

Instructions regarding War Diaries and Intelligence Summaries are contained in F. S. Regs., Part II. and the Staff Manual respectively. Title Pages will be prepared in manuscript.

Place	Date	Hour	Summary of Events and Information	Remarks and references to Appendices
	Monday Aug 9th		Standing in general bombardment at 2am in the morning did good work by firing 1½ inch and 1½ 2 inch bombs, in the afternoon engaged for day into near 1½ inch gun emplacement	
	Tuesday 10th	11.30 am	fired hint 39 firs in reply to enemy trench bombing them on the enemy trenches and observed them from us. Visited the Westerns attached to 138th Bde. in the afternoon.	
	Wednesday 11th	12.45 am	replied to German bombs by front + 80/m north the closest result. Also fired 2 more light bombs at	
		3.15 am	replying to bombardment. Visited the detachments with the 138th Bde. At 9/pm fired 3 light + heavy 1½ inch bombs	
	Thursday 12th	1.33/pm at 12.45 am	when stopped the enemy from shelling our lines bomb. Fired 8 rounds at day. rest in the evening with considerable damage done. In reply to enemies in front of the enemy during the night. 9 hyper bombs were fired.	

WAR DIARY
or
INTELLIGENCE SUMMARY

(Erase heading not required.)

Army Form C. 2118

Place	Date	Hour	Summary of Events and Information	Remarks and references to Appendices
	Friday 13th			
	Saturday 14		On anglA for a new position for the 2 inch Howitzer. No firing of any consequence. Tried 2 16hr driving rings which were both air burst, 18" gun found and took charge on position of German m.g.s, fired on it with 2" a.r ? A.P, but did not silence it owing to using up all the ammunition shortly and is very accurate. Tried with railway cutting with desired effect	
	Sunday 15			

WAR DIARY
or
INTELLIGENCE SUMMARY

Army Form C. 2118

41 ?? How Bty

Place	Date	Hour	Summary of Events and Information	Remarks and references to Appendices
Monday	16th August		Situation quiet. Three heavy bombs 1½ inch fired in the evening with excellent results.	
Tuesday	17th		21 Dardnell worked the trench howitzers attached to 138th Inf Brigade whilst observing rounds fired by the heavy howitzers. He received a bullet wound in the neck.	
Wednesday	18th		I came up to trenches from billets in the morning. In the afternoon went out to see the guns with 138th Bde. Afterwards fired 8 rounds. It was at enemy's loopholes, showing inaccurate owing to bed being loose.	
Thursday	19th		Rearranged the beds of the guns attached to 137th Bde. Fired two rounds in the evening in reply to German bomb, but exploding on the crest of the hill.	
Friday	20th		Returned to billets to arrange for withdrawal of rifles, grenades and distribution of infantry who have been put to use. New artillery officer arrived. At night I returned to trenches of 138th Bde.	
Saturday	21st		Enemy very busy, using Lager machine gun against trenches of 137th Bde. Replied with expre and also with 15 inch gun.	
Sunday	22nd		Situation quiet. No rounds fired during day	

26/9/15 J O Lavery Lieut R.G.A
for O.C. 41st Trench Howitzer Battery

WAR DIARY
or
INTELLIGENCE SUMMARY

(Erase heading not required.)

Army Form C. 2118

XLVI
41: 777 74/55

Place	Date	Hour	Summary of Events and Information	Remarks and references to Appendices
Thursday	Aug 23		137ᵗʰ R.G.A. fired 2-33pm and 1-18pm from No 2 gun. All duds	
Tuesday	24ᵗʰ		All quiet	
Wednesday	25ᵗʰ		About 10 pm Boche fired a few T.M. bombs into 38 Trench. Replied with 2 35pm from No 1 gun and 2-18pm from No 2 gun, which silenced enemy mortars. Result No 1 – 1 Hit, No 2 – 1 Hit, 2 Blinds, 2 Gun bursts	
Thursday	26ᵗʰ		Infantry preparing emplacement at 35 left for 1ᵗʰ inch gun. Ordered spare bed up from Hilda. (2) 5ᵗʰ S. Staffords promised to have it brought up from Dunraven.	
Friday	27ᵗʰ		Fired 6-33pm and 3-18pm at 2pm. While the Heavy Trench guns were firing, 5 Heavy and one light went duds and one light burst. Placed spare bed in Trench 35.	
Saturday	28ᵗʰ		All quiet	
Sunday	29ᵗʰ		All quiet	

J.P. Lavery
Lieut R.G.A.
for O.C. 41ˢᵗ I. H. Bty

WAR DIARY
or
INTELLIGENCE SUMMARY
(Erase heading not required.)

Army Form C. 2118

41ˢᵗ ˢⁿ / Ab. Bty

Place	Date	Hour	Summary of Events and Information	Remarks and references to Appendices
Monday	30ᵗʰ Aug			
Tuesday	31ˢᵗ		Nothing to report	
Wednesday	1ˢᵗ Sept			
Thursday	2ⁿᵈ		Went to Divisional Headquarters for pay	
Friday	3ʳᵈ		Transferred men to new billets	
Saturday	4ᵗʰ		Went to trench 34 to arrange for new position for 1st sect. Issued 2 bombs '8's in reply to German trench bomb. BMs chucks	
Sunday	5ᵗʰ		Tried up new lot in trench 34.	

9ᵗʰ Lowry 42 N.I.A
for O.C. 41ˢᵗ T. H. Bty

WAR DIARY or INTELLIGENCE SUMMARY

Army Form C. 2118

4¹ᵗ Trench Mortar Bty

(Erase heading not required.)

Instructions regarding War Diaries and Intelligence Summaries are contained in F.S. Regs., Part II. and the Staff Manual respectively. Title Pages will be prepared in manuscript.

Place	Date	Hour	Summary of Events and Information	Remarks and references to Appendices
Monday	Sept 13ᵗʰ		Came up to trenches in the evening	
Tuesday	Sept 14ᵗʰ		Fired two registering rounds out of 4 inch mm. Day spent in repairing dugout.	
Wednesday	Sept 15ᵗʰ		30 rounds 1.5 pr ammunition arrived. Arranged a bed for 1.5 inch gun in trench 35. One round 2 inch fired at night silenced the enemy's fire.	
Thursday	Sept 16ᵗʰ		Altered bed of 1.5 inch in trench 34.	
Friday	Sept 17ᵗʰ		Fired seven rounds 1.5 inch in the afternoon as Russ mortar failing from being shaky and two air howitzers. In the evening a severe bombardment of our trenches took place, during which the 1.5 inch gun in trench 38 was destroyed.	
Saturday	Sept 18ᵗʰ		Prepared a new emplacement in left sector to replace emplacement destroyed, and put in a new bed.	
Sunday	Sept 19ᵗʰ		Fired 2 50 prs in reply to German trench mortars bombs. Both air bursts.	A 239/9/15

J. Harvey 2/Lt R.F.A.
for O.C. 41ⁿᵈ Trench Mortar Bty

WAR DIARY
or
INTELLIGENCE SUMMARY

Army Form C. 2118

4th Trench Mortar ... [Bty]

Place	Date	Hour	Summary of Events and Information	Remarks and references to Appendices
Houdain	27th Sept		Ammunition arrived in billets at 11p.m. Went up to trenches, bringing ammunition as far as Transport Farm.	
Tuesday	28th		Ammunition brought up to trenches in the evening by infantry fatigue party.	
Wednesday	29th		Nothing to report. Schrabim very quiet.	
Thursday	30th		Enemy blew up a mine in trench 35 and followed with active bombardment. We replied with 10 1½ inch bombs.	
Friday	1st Oct		Two more mines blown up by enemy in trench 39. Schrabim quiet.	
Saturday	2nd Oct		Enemy busy with trench mortars on the crater in trench 39. Replied with 1½ inch bombs at intervals on the parapets opposite.	
Sunday	3rd Oct		Schrabim quiet during the day. In the evening he threw over heavy rifle grenade mortars. We replied with 6 bombs, which kept the enemy quiet for some time.	

Jo Kenny Lt R.G.A.
for O.C. 4/1st Trench Mortar Bty.

Army Form C. 2118

WAR DIARY
or
INTELLIGENCE SUMMARY
41st [Trench?] Mortar [Battery?]
(Erase heading not required.)

Instructions regarding War Diaries and Intelligence Summaries are contained in F.S. Regs., Part II. and the Staff Manual respectively. Title Pages will be prepared in manuscript.

Place	Date	Hour	Summary of Events and Information	Remarks and references to Appendices
Monday	11th	Oct	Nothing to report.	
Tuesday	12th		Prepared to hurry but no lights thrown	
Wednesday	13th		About to attack at request of infantry front 5 rounds from 37. Friends of which 4 were duds	
Thursday	14th		Fired 4 rounds from 35 S. All duds.	
Friday	15th		Fired 2 rounds from 37. Both thuds. Also fired for guns in trench 38, an SOS on our front trench received	
Saturday	16th		Fired 7 rounds from the early morning in reply to German trench mortars. One had no influence. Kept most in trench 36. Germans acted with trench mortars through the night.	
Sunday	17th		10 rounds fired last night & in the early part of the morning. One thrown but failed to burst in trench 38.	

Oct 17th

J. [Kenny?] Lt R.G.A.
For O.C. 41st Trench Mortar Battery

R 27/15

WAR DIARY or INTELLIGENCE SUMMARY

Army Form C. 2118

4th Trench Mortar Battery

Place	Date	Hour	Summary of Events and Information	Remarks and references to Appendices
Monday	25th Oct		Six rounds fired at emplacement opposite trench 37, causing much damage to the parapet.	
Tuesday	26th Oct		Much rain falling, both sides quiet. Nothing to report.	
Wednesday	27th Oct		Nothing to report, situation quiet.	
Thursday	28th Oct		Early this morning a shell fell in dug-out in trench 38 killing one gunner and wounding two privates of the Argyll & Sutherland Highlanders. Twelve rounds fired in trench 37 several trenches reached rapidly on the enemy's parapets. New relief came in the evening.	
Friday	29th Oct		An organised bombardment by trench mortars arranged to draw the fire & hence locate position of enemy minenwerfer which has been active the previous week. We fired 15 heavy and 16 light from two guns on – trench 37 and one – trench 35. doing much damage to enemy trench especially from gun in trench 35, which enfilade about 50 yards of the enemy trench. We failed, however, to draw enough fire for minenwerfer.	
Saturday	30th Oct		Two rounds fired this morning otherwise all quiet.	
Sunday	31st Oct		Situation quiet. Went to trench 41 to reconnoitre two position for gun emplacements. Was wherefore trajectoire chancelier by man & battalion which is been entered the trenches, but was soon identified.	

J Phaverry Lieut. R.G.A.
for O.C. 4th Trench Mortar Battery

Nov 2nd 1915

WAR DIARY
or
INTELLIGENCE SUMMARY

(Erase heading not required.)

Army Form C. 2118

41st Trench Mortar Battery

Place	Date	Hour	Summary of Events and Information	Remarks and references to Appendices
Monday	15th	Noon	Situation normal	
Tuesday	16th		Returned from leave, entered the trenches in the evening. The rain of the previous week helped to make the contrast between home comforts and trench discomforts very pronounced.	
Wednesday	17th		Have been working on a new Mortar dugout, which is in an old cellar requiring first to be cleared of debris. Heavy showers and aeroplanes have sin the work.	
Thursday	18th		Work continued on dug-out.	
Friday	19th		Rebuilt a bomb store in trench 36, which had fallen in at the back owing to heavy rain.	
Saturday	20th		New emplacement made for 2 inch gun, but much water found the next moment to have soaked through the fields. Looking around for next position. The officers' dug-out completed except for the roof. Materials not yet arrived from the R.E.	
Sunday	21st		Improved gun emplacement in trench 37 and showed 36 by means of the trench fronts.	

Sunday 21st Jan 1915

Johansey 21 A.G.A.
41st Trench Mortar Battery

Army Form C. 2118

WAR DIARY
or
INTELLIGENCE SUMMARY
(Erase heading not required.)

4th Jewish AntiAircraft Battery

Instructions regarding War Diaries and Intelligence Summaries are contained in F. S. Regs., Part II. and the Staff Manual respectively. Title Pages will be prepared in manuscript.

Place	Date	Hour	Summary of Events and Information	Remarks and references to Appendices
Monday	Nov 22nd		Commenced to dig a trench for new emplacement — trench 38.	
Tuesday	" 23rd		Completed new emplacement — trench 38.	
Wednesday	" 24th		Fired 7 registering rounds, 3 g white fumes to explore, 3 direct damage to the parapets on the hill. The accuracy in which seven shells burst a commendation feat which we were good.	
Thursday	" 25th		Cut a reliable trench for better protection of the men.	
Friday	" 26th		Completed bomb place in trench 38.	
Saturday	" 27th		8 rounds fires from trench 37 on opposite trenches. Burst on slopes, first failed to explore & two slightly over the parapets.	
Sunday	" 28th		New heavy dugout howitzer gun emplacement.	

Nov 28th 1915

J.O. Harvey, Lieut R.H.A.

WAR DIARY
or
INTELLIGENCE SUMMARY

(Erase heading not required.)

Army Form C. 2118

W⁴⁵ Trench Mortar Battery.

Place	Date	Hour	Summary of Events and Information	Remarks and references to Appendices
	29/4/16		Went to Trenches in early morning, found what it was G.O.C. wished to get rid of, & also if I wanted more sent up. Stated I wished to be jolly.	
	29/4/16		Was called at at 2.30 A.M. by infantry & requested to fire a few rounds & Germans were very active. Fired three 33/4" at Random fort. Was being offensive in enemy's trench. He also being active. Was asked to retaliate again at 4.30 A.M. Fired 4 33/4" which stopped them. One was a silent round. In spite of the other rounds we could not be observed owing to thick mist. Commanding officer later called at office later in day, & cordially thanked us for our support. Gunnister being of assistance. Officer in charge went to the Random fort in the afternoon. Took an inventory of kit. Stores now taken over by us.	
	30/4/16		At 7 P.M. took advantage of moonlight for a bit of re- taliation. Fired 12 rounds of heavy trench mortar on the enemy trenches. Received letter testifying to the value of our work in retaliation in cooperation with infantry. Also infantry C.O. permitted us to billet 9 men in farm to which we have to advance. Also infantry engineers sent 10 badges of sandbags for emergency.	

WAR DIARY
or
INTELLIGENCE SUMMARY

(Erase heading not required.)

Army Form C. 2118

Instructions regarding War Diaries and Intelligence Summaries are contained in F.S. Regs., Part II. and the Staff Manual respectively. Title Pages will be prepared in manuscript.

Place	Date	Hour	Summary of Events and Information	Remarks and references to Appendices
	1/10/15		the following day. Continued working on Dug-out (4 ours) which was commenced Nov 11 & I successfully destroyed by a Shell. Rustic reinforcement to Tunnel 28. Put 2 faints pointing at T 29.C. tube. Carried up 50 ℔ tubes from Railway Dug-out to Anvil Store. Commenced construction of Bomb Store at greenhouses material above surface water. Continued working up for Officers dug-out & dug a drain from same to carry away surface water.	
	2/10/15		Carried Infantry material from Railway Dug-out to Storage by working day and night. Carrieties wounded in head by Shrapnel. 8 sappers dug out Road above at 2 enhancement arm/dua. Feed slabs - 33 of two & two 18 ft deep at intervals during the day at joints in enemy trenches where machine guns so believed to be located, & succeeded in registering hits on trenches which caused extensive damage to parapet. Seven 13 ℔ tubes and one 18 ℔ tube were blinds.	
	3/10/15		Rain fell during the greater part of the day & flooded entrances to Tunnels 27,9 up to Red G. Called across drainage was impossible. Roof of 9 mens dug-out leaking badly & I caused it will shed of covering as in 9 and dug-out.	

WAR DIARY
or
INTELLIGENCE SUMMARY

(Erase heading not required.)

Army Form C. 2118

Place	Date	Hour	Summary of Events and Information	Remarks and references to Appendices
	4/3/16 (cont)		Fired eight 33½lbs during artillery bombardment and make four likes or propt. Two of the rounds were blind.	
	5/3/16		Riveted expansion track 37 in M. Salley's unsupported alpine during the night, the rest of the men being on officer's depot. Relieved at 7:30 P.M.	

C Kinsete
J.C. R.G.A.
41st Trench Mortar by

Army Form C. 2118

12/12/15

1st Trench Mortar Battery

WAR DIARY
or
INTELLIGENCE SUMMARY
(Erase heading not required.)

Instructions regarding War Diaries and Intelligence Summaries are contained in F. S. Regs, Part II. and the Staff Manual respectively. Title Pages will be prepared in manuscript.

Place	Date	Hour	Summary of Events and Information	Remarks and references to Appendices
G. 92 Central.	Dec 6.		The 15" Emplacement in Trench 37 was completed and bed laid satisfactorily, also the 2" position in Scottish Trench was repaired as the sides were continually slipping. Message was received from O.C. Trench Mortars 9th Div. to the effect that an Scherer had been worked out by which the Mortars were to bombard several points of enemy's trench in conjunction with the Artillery. A 2" gun was accordingly laid on T29 C 0.4 9, two 15"guns on pts T29 C 7.0.	
	Dec 7.		New emplacements for 2nd day were completed in evening.	
	Dec 8.		Sappers were laid from 2" gun to Observation Post in front of trench. Ran his during greater part of day.	
	Dec 9.		Six Mortars fired in the morning in reply to German Trench Mortars, two of which burst in the air, the others drifted on & after exploded there. At 12.30 P.M. fired two 2" bombs on certain working together with 11.33/4 & 5.18/4 div. No direct hits were obtained though several bombs fell on enemy's parapets. A little stress the bed started to sink owing to softness of ground.	
	Dec 10.		I came in trench last evening until relief. Baled out emplacement in Trench 37 as it had been flooded during the night, but on getting the water down found the water to be bubbling up through the ground as there	

Army Form C. 2118

WAR DIARY
or
INTELLIGENCE SUMMARY
(Erase heading not required.)

Instructions regarding War Diaries and Intelligence Summaries are contained in F. S. Regs., Part II. and the Staff Manual respectively. Title Pages will be prepared in manuscript.

Place	Date	Hour	Summary of Events and Information	Remarks and references to Appendices
	Dec 11.		was no roof of hutting it water was certilled to clear the position. Repaired roof of men's dug out which was leaking badly. Commenced construction of platform of branch & timber under 2" gun, as bed had sunk badly during previous shoot owing to ground being soft & spongy. Cleaned out Trench round about 13 emplacement Infantry he leys & Birkenhead huts as these also had sunk considerably. Got at Ninety 33 lbdrs. together with two 18 Rds & two 2" New Patt Rds bolts away. Stores from Trenchart Farm to Railway Cottage.	Reg
	Dec 12.		Laid 2" gun on new platform & commenced building Rock Stove at this position. Relaid the two 18 lbds in Trench 35 & carried up 30 heavy bomb from cutting. C. Kinston 2/Lt R.G.A.	

Army Form C. 2118

WAR DIARY
or
INTELLIGENCE SUMMARY
(Erase heading not required.)

4th French Mortar Battery

Instructions regarding War Diaries and Intelligence Summaries are contained in F. S. Regs., Part II. and the Staff Manual respectively. Title Pages will be prepared in manuscript.

Place	Date	Hour	Summary of Events and Information	Remarks and references to Appendices
Monday	Dec 13th		Carried up 25 2 inch bombs to trenches in afternoon to shoot in the afternoon. Relaid telephone wire to O.P. to communication trench H.Q headquarters	
Tuesday	Dec 14th		Fired Registration 2 inch and another 33 from communication. The observing was quite successful but no thing hands in enemy lines. The observing was quite successful a lot cover available though kept close to the doorways stone pinnk. On one occasion two Zeppelins were noticed after our 2 inch bombs was fired. After the third round of 2 inch the 2nd shell became + we was hastily put in at the shooting Continued	
Wednesday	Dec 15th		Remounted hatch 47 S.T. for positions from which to happy/k I.G.O.3.7. Started to Canny all 2 inch Stokes 6 batting to accordance with an order which was afterwards cancelled. Sound 2 inch open as I.G.O.3.2.6 had returned instruction 4 have there. Returned to Transport Farm to lay up 20 2 inch bombs	
Thursday	Dec 16th		Find me 2 inch in hand I.G.O.2. and about 100 trip standard nuns to kit/stores were travelling down. Also find 1/2 2 33pn at I.G.O.7.t.t. Have been very efficient.	
Friday	Dec 17th		8 4th In duties like Released at 5 pm Took up 12 2 inch bs from Hooges barrel tramway was suspended in 41 S to supply to I.G.O.3.7. Checked the stores in the men's dryout.	
Saturday	Dec 18th		Men supplement bayptios to hospital as laid. Three horse officers of divisional division took up and inspected the gun positions dryout.	

1875 Wt. W593/826 1,000,000 4/15 J.B.C. & A. (A.D.S.S./Forms/C. 2118.)

WAR DIARY
or
INTELLIGENCE SUMMARY

Army Form C. 2118

Instructions regarding War Diaries and Intelligence Summaries are contained in F. S. Regs., Part II. and the Staff Manual respectively. Title Pages will be prepared in manuscript.

(Erase heading not required.)

Place	Date	Hour	Summary of Events and Information	Remarks and references to Appendices
Sunday	Dec 19	19th	Early this morning enemy commenced a heavy bombardment. Got the men up to the guns and commenced firing on hostile points. Two rounds had fired from the 2 inch when it was noticed that the bed plate was badly severely fractured down to the wood. 5 rounds 15 inch were also fired, but firing was slow owing to the friction tubes being very tight fit. Rest in an old pattern which has in place of the one used in the morning very heavy bombardment in the afternoon. Got the new mortars in a convenient place to the 1½ inch german trench 38.	

Dec 19

J. Lowery Lieut RGA
J.S.C. 4th Trench Mortar Battery

WAR DIARY
or
INTELLIGENCE SUMMARY

(Erase heading not required.)

Army Form C. 2118.

XIV 41/1 T.M.B.

Vol 1-2+3

Place	Date	Hour	Summary of Events and Information	Remarks and references to Appendices
	8/3/16		The Battery left 3rd Army T.M School and proceeded by train to Saulty, and marched to Sivrencourt. There halted for the night. T.M.B	
	9/3/16		Left Sivrencourt 10.30 marched to Arras and reported to 41st Bgde HQ. T.M.B	
	10/3/16		Reconnoitred positions for Mortars in Blangy and St Sauveur Sectors. T.M.B	
	11/3/16		One gun and detachment occupied Cellar in Blangy. T.M.B	
	13/3/16		Another gun and detachment sent to St Sauveur Sector. T.M.B	
	15/3/16		Fired 15 rounds at Sap opposite I 49. at 230 yds T.M.B	
	16/3/16		Fired 19 rounds at Sap opposite I 5. at 380 yds. T.M.B	
	17/3/16		Relief sent down to Blangy. T.M.B	
	18/3/16		Fired 4 rounds at Sap opposite I 49. at 230 yds T.M.B	
	19/3/16		Relief sent down to St Sauveur. T.M.B	
	21/3/16		Reconnoitred for O.P in Blangy. T.M.B	
	23/3/16		Established Trench HQ in Blangy. Both detachments relieved. T.M.B	
	25/3/16		Changed Trench HQ to Gillard next to K.R.R. HQ. T.M.B	
	29/3/16		Both detachments relieved, and brought up another gun to position right of the Arras Foully railway to reach PT 213 m German lines. T.M.B	

T.A. Ballock Lieut
OC 41/1 T.M.B.

WAR DIARY
or
INTELLIGENCE SUMMARY.

Army Form C. 2118.

(Erase heading not required.)

Place	Date	Hour	Summary of Events and Information	Remarks and references to Appendices
A.A.	2/4/16		Fired 5 rounds at Mushroom House Blangy at 380508. TAB	
	5/4/16		Both detachments relieved. TAB	
	6/4/16		Fired 15 rounds round Mushroom House and Enemy 2nd line trenches at ranges from 430–460 in retaliation for Enemy Vans Bombs & Rifle Grenades. TAB	
	7/4/16		2.P. Oakey raises the Bty for Special coy RE at Helfast TAB	
	8/4/16		Enemy retaliated on 60pdr. T. Mortars X14 Bty. Fired 1 round in retaliation. Owing to a bad strike no more rounds could be fired. TAB	
	9/4/16		Fired 8 rounds in retaliation to Enemy Mortar. X14 Bty fired 13 rounds making a total of 21 rounds to Enemy 7. 2/Lt A/Sgt Oakes in charge in the Trenches. TAB	
	13/4/16		Received W/n from II Corps not to fire at a great range than 300yds East in an emergency. TAB	
	15/4/16		The Bty is reinforced by a Res Bty of 5 NCO 16 Rfn. TAB	
	16/4/16		Both Detachments relieved. 7 rounds fired at Enemy Sap S of Arras. TAB	
	17/4/16		Relieve A/Sgt Oakes in Trenches TAB. S of Arras – Cambrai Railway.	

WAR DIARY
or
INTELLIGENCE SUMMARY.

(Erase heading not required.)

Army Form C. 2118.

Instructions regarding War Diaries and Intelligence Summaries are contained in F. S. Regs., Part II. and the Staff Manual respectively. Title pages will be prepared in manuscript.

Place	Date	Hour	Summary of Events and Information	Remarks and references to Appendices
	18/4/16		XIV T.M. Bty opened fire on new enemy work opposite 151-1.50. Enemy mortars fired in retaliation. For this Tr. 2 mortars of XIV Bty and 1 mortar of this Bty retaliated. The latter firing 14 rounds at the mushroom and enemy 2nd line to the right of it. T.A.B.	
	19/4/16.		N.C.O. 6 men sent up to the three positions for instruction, belongs to Res. Bty. T.A.B.	
	20/4/16.		2nd R.W. Eyton Jones the Bty from off a course at 3rd Army School. T.A.B.	
	22/4/16	4pm	Fired 4 rounds at 50-year mound opposite 1.52. T.A.B.	
	23/4/16		All detachments retained. T.A.B.	
	24/4/16		2nd R. Eyton takes over Trench H.Q. T.A.B.	
	25/4/16	4 a.m.	Enemy "rum jar" type of mortars, starting firing on our front line, more especially on the Boiler House, Blangy Xia Bty and No. 3 6in. retaliated with 15 & 10 rounds respectively. Ditcham's for No. 3 Gun moved to a dugout in 115 line. T.A.B.	
	27/4/16		All detachments relieved. T.A.B.	
	29/4/16		Fired 9 rounds in registration on Sap X opposite 1.50 Trench from new gun position. Swivel didn't hit vases. Second T.A.B.	
	30/4/16			

41/1 T.M. Bty

Army Form C. 2118.

WAR DIARY
or
INTELLIGENCE SUMMARY.
(Erase heading not required.)

Place	Date	Hour	Summary of Events and Information	Remarks and references to Appendices
Field	4.5.16		Removed M Bty from trenches to Reserve Billets in Arras R.o.F.	
	7.5.16		T/A Baldock 2Lt proceeds on a course to Hesdin. R.o.F. Lt Lm 2Lt takes command of the Bty. R.o.F.	
	9.5.16		Bty moves to Warlus. R.o.F.	
	10.5.16		Bty moves to billets in Aubigny. R.o.F.	
	17.5.16		Inspection of Bty by Brig Gen Steavenson C.O. 41st Inf. Bgde at the billets. R.o.F.	
	22.5.16		Bty moves up to billets in Bois du Flaux, Mt St Eloi. R.o.F.	
	24.5.16		C.D.H. Vaughan 2Lt having joined is posted to the Res Bty. (attached to 41/1 T.M.B.) on 15.4.16). R.o.F.	
	31.5.16		A Res. Personnel consisting of one Officer C.E.SS. Eccles 2Lt, 1 Sergeant, 2 Corpl's and 10 R/n is attached to the Bty. after a course at 3rd Army School. R.o.F.	

CONFIDENTIAL.

WAR DIARY

- of -

41st TRENCH MORTAR BATTERY.

From: 1st July, 1916.
To: 31st " 1916.

Volume V.

Army Form C. 2118.

WAR DIARY
or
INTELLIGENCE SUMMARY.
(Erase heading not required.)

Instructions regarding War Diaries and Intelligence Summaries are contained in F. S. Regs., Part II. and the Staff Manual respectively. Title pages will be prepared in manuscript.

Place	Date	Hour	Summary of Events and Information	Remarks and references to Appendices
Fn'b	1st		Considerable firing in retaliation for enemy mortars all diary month, firing on us about 120 rounds a day. All light guns remain in action. TMB	
"	2nd	11.10 pm	Mine was sprung at 118 Crater. Enemy opened just a slight bombardment to which we retaliated. Two guns were firing just over the Crater. Soon after it had gone up. TMB	
"	3rd to 23rd (inclusive)		General Retaliation for Enemy mortars TMB	
"	24th	3.30	Measured bombardment by 4.5, 18 pdr, 2in Mortars & Stokes on divided front	
"		4.30	Emplacements and loopholes in enemy front line. It appears very effective though the retaliation was not heavy. The Battery fired over 500 rounds TMB	
"	25th – 28th (inclusive)		As from 3rd to 23rd TMB Total rounds fired during month approximate to 3,000 rounds approx TMB	
"	29th	11am 12noon	Battery relieved about 11am. by 64th T.M. Battery. TMB	
"	30th	9.0 p.m.	The Battery was transported by lorry to GRAND ROULLECOURT, leaving Arras 9 p.m. TMB	

1577 Wt.W10791/1773 500,000 1/15 D. D. & L. A.D.S.S./Forms/C. 2118.

CONFIDENTIAL.

WAR DIARY

- of -

41st TRENCH MORTAR BATTERY.

From: 1st August, 1916 - To: 31st August, 1916.

Volume VI.

Army Form C. 2118.

WAR DIARY
or
INTELLIGENCE SUMMARY.
(Erase heading not required.)

Instructions regarding War Diaries and Intelligence Summaries are contained in F.S. Regs., Part II. and the Staff Manual respectively. Title pages will be prepared in manuscript.

Place	Date	Hour	Summary of Events and Information	Remarks and references to Appendices
	1/8/16	8.15	Marched from OCOCHES to GEZAINCOURT. TMy	
	7/8/16	4 pm	Marched from GEZAINCOURT to CANDAS stations and thence entrained about 11 p.m.	
	8/8/16	8 am	Detrained at CORBIE and marched to billets at DERNANCOURT TMy	
	10/8/16		Reconnoitred the bed. by 50th Bde. TMy	
	12/8/16	6.30 pm	Left billets at DERNANCOURT and arrived at POZIERES REDOUBT TMy	
	13/8/16	4 am	Relief carried out with 50. T.M. B5. 4 mortars in CARLTON TRENCH remainder at POZIERES REDOUBT. 7Ay	
		8 am		
	18/8/16	2.45 pm	5 mortars in action in support of infantry attack on ORCHARD TRENCH & WOOD LANE. All mortars fired for 5 minutes a/ZERO. and 2 in kept up a barrage on FLERS Rd. as long as ammunition would last. About 500 rounds fired. Remaining 3 mortars in reserve CARLTON TRENCH. TMy	
	19/8/16 night		B5 relieved by 105th T.M. B5. and in turn we relieved 43rd T.M. B5. in DELVILLE WOOD. TMy	
	19/20			
	21/8/16	4.30 pm	Fired in support of an minor enterprise in DELVILLE WOOD. About 300 rounds fired. 5 mortars in action. TMy	
	22/8/16	2.45 pm	4 pts T.M. B5 changes places with 42 T.M. B5. 2 guns in action, remainder to rest in Bethon Villers on HOPL	

WAR DIARY
or
INTELLIGENCE SUMMARY.
(Erase heading not required.)

Army Form C. 2118.

Place	Date	Hour	Summary of Events and Information	Remarks and references to Appendices
in vic.	24/8/16	2.45 pm	4 guns fired on HOP ALLEY, in support of infantry attack. One put out by bomb jamming down muzzle. 2 non-mortars burnd. About 160 rounds fired.	
	26/8/16	6.30-7	Fired 30 rounds in support of bombing attack by D.L.I. Operations cancelled at half time.	
	28/8/16	4.am.	Relieved by the 22nd T.M. Bg. and proceeded to DERNANCOURT.	
	30/8/16	12 am	Marched to ALBERT and there entrained about 4 pm. Detrained at ARRAISNES 10 pm and marched to COCIGNY.	

www.ingramcontent.com/pod-product-compliance
Lightning Source LLC
Chambersburg PA
CBHW081501160426
43193CB00013B/2552